AN ALBUM
OF CHINESE
AMERICANS

AN ALBUM OF
Chinese Americans

BY BETTY LEE SUNG

FRANKLIN WATTS | NEW YORK | LONDON | 1977

Graphs on pages 29 and 30,
courtesy of Betty Lee Sung,
drawn by Vantage Art, Inc.

Cover photograph by Corky Lee.

Photographs courtesy of:
Emil Bocian, *China Post:* pages 36 (left), 37, 46 (top), 50, 53 (left), 54 (top), 57 (bottom); Corky Lee: frontispiece, pages 38, 40 (right), 46 (bottom), 53 (right), 54 (bottom), 58; California Historical Society: page 6; State Archives of Hawaii: page 8 (top); Library of Congress: pages 16 (right), 20, 26; Bernice P. Bishop Museum: page 8 (bottom); *Jade* magazine: page 11; San Francisco Public Library: pages 12, 13, 19; Southern Pacific: pages 15, 16 (left); New York Historical Society: pages 19, 25 (right); The National Archives: page 22; Joseph Chin: page 51; American Airlines: page 24; Housing and Development Administration (The City of New York): page 42; Arthur Horn: page 32; Hawaii Visitors Bureau: page 44; John Leong: page 25 (left); Robert Young: page 33 (bottom); Sam Reiss, *New York Teacher:* page 33 (top); Richard Kramer: page 34; Chung L. Lo: page 36 (right); Kem Lee Studio: page 61 (bottom); Empress of China, San Francisco: page 40 (left); Boreysa Tep: page 41; United Press International: page 59; Matt Tomasulo: page 57 (top); CBS News: page 62 (bottom left); Charles Chao: page 61 (top left); U.S. Air Force: page 61 (top right); Museum of Modern Art/Film Stills Archive: page 62 (top right).

Library of Congress Cataloging in Publication Data

Sung, Betty Lee.
    An album of the Chinese Americans.

    Includes index.
    SUMMARY: Discusses the life of Chinese Americans today including their past history and their present customs and problems.
    1. Chinese Americans—Social life and customs—Juvenile literature. 2. Chinese Americans—History—Juvenile literature. [1. Chinese Americans] I. Title.
E184.C5S937   301.45'19'51073   76–45185
ISBN 0–531–00366–3

CONTENTS

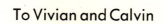

To Vivian and Calvin

AN ALBUM OF CHINESE AMERICANS

Instead of panning for gold dust, the Chinese devised a much more effective contraption called the sluice box or "long tom." Sand or gravel was shoveled into the trough, which had grooves at the bottom. The swift-running waters from the top washed away the sand, trapping the gold dust in the grooves.

CHINESE FORE-BEARS

When we think about the birth of this nation, we think about Christopher Columbus, the *Mayflower* landing, and the pilgrims. We tend to forget that the United States has a western coast and that this region was settled long before Columbus ever set foot on American soil.

In fact, there is strong evidence that people from China had settled in the Americas over 2,500 years ago. They probably set sail in double canoes, plank boats, or rafts and were carried by strong ocean currents that brought them to these western shores.

Scientists, who have studied Indian cultures in the Pacific Northwest, in Mexico, and in Peru see a definite Chinese influence in the calendar, the arts, and the tools of the American Indians. The strongest link lies in the race of the American Indians. Both American Indians and Chinese belong to the Mongolian race. In short, the earliest native Americans may have been Chinese.

Few people like to think of the settlement of the American continents this way. There are no exact records, and the settlements established along the West Coast are long gone. Only the ruins of the Indian civilizations give us some clues.

However, we do know for certain that the Chinese were among the pioneer settlers of the American West. They came to California when gold was discovered in 1848. The news of gold had traveled to Canton, a southern port city in China, almost before word reached the eastern shores of the United States. The Chinese were among the "forty-niners" who rushed here in ships, in the same way as brave and adventurous men from all over the world. These early pioneers risked life and limb in the hope of finding gold.

The Chinese came in clipper ships with big billowy sails. When there was a good strong wind, the ships moved rapidly through the waters. Even then, the journey across the Pacific Ocean sometimes took as long as three months.

The first Chinese settlers landed near San Francisco, where gold

Shown here are some of the first Chinese immigrants on board a ship bound for the New World. The hair style, decreed by the Manchu emperor for the men at that time, was to shave the forehead and wear a pigtail.

A Chinese family in front of their home in the midst of the Hawaiian sugarcane fields where they work. The first Chinese arrived in Hawaii in 1852. They were recruited as contract laborers for the sugar plantations.

had been discovered. They came from a vast empire with a recorded history of over 4,670 years. China is a country as big as the United States today, but in spite of its vast size, it had more people than it could feed. When the land cannot support the people, some of them have to go elsewhere. Most people do not like to leave their country and go to unknown lands, but the prospect of getting rich quick was a special reason.

PIONEERS OF THE WEST

The word "gold" not only attracted the Chinese, but lured men from all corners of the globe. They came from France, Spain, Mexico, Chile, Peru, Russia, Australia, and, of course, from the eastern states of the United States. Within a few short years, the hills where Mexican sheepherders once tended their flocks were swarming with swashbuckling men, all hoping to become rich overnight. This period in American history is called the Gold Rush.

By the year 1870, one out of every four people who had flocked to California was Chinese. By and large, these immigrants were young men from the poorer families living in and around the region of Canton. They came with the intent of working hard, saving their money, and going back to China. They did not bring their wives or children with them.

These men came with a dream of finding gold, so it was natural that they would turn to mining. But the burden of a tax on foreign miners fell very heavily upon the Chinese. They looked different — more foreign than the other foreigners. Usually they had to pay the tax while white foreign miners escaped payment. As a result, the Chinese turned to fishing, farming, manufacturing, and drainage work. They harvested the land and the sea to provide food for the increasing numbers who continued to stream West. Theirs were the hands that stitched shoes and clothes and provided the services so vitally needed on the western frontier.

[9]

Some of the first Chinese to come east were these workers recruited to make shoes in North Adams, Massachusetts, in 1870.

A Chinese kitchen preserved from early mining days at California. Note the "wok" and many-layered steamer set into the brick stove. Both cooking utensils found their way into American kitchens when it was discovered how efficient they were.

Facing page: Chinese women in the United States were a rare sight back in the days when the U.S. flag had only a few stars (see upper left corner of photo). Note the elaborate embroidery of the ladies' skirts and jackets. Above left: there were few Chinese children in the early history of Chinese settlements in the United States. The ones who were here were dressed in traditional silks and embroideries. Above right: by the turn of the century, American styles were adopted.

BUILDING THE RAILROAD

The West grew very rapidly, but it was separated from the eastern states by a vast stretch of land and was beyond the reach of rivers or waterways or roads. Much of this expanse was not part of the United States yet. Some of the territory was under Mexican influence, and other parts were under Spanish, British, or French control. The U.S. Congress was very afraid that the North American continent might be split up into tiny countries like those in Europe or South America. To tie the country together, Congress voted in 1861 to build a railroad that would go across the continent from the Atlantic Ocean to the Pacific Ocean. The common means of transportation then were horseback and covered wagon. Just to get a message from Washington, D.C., to San Francisco took weeks or even months.

The contracts to build the railroad were given to the Union Pacific, which was to build westward from Omaha, Nebraska, and the Central Pacific, which was to build eastward from Sacramento, California. The rails were to link up and form one continuous line, tying in with existing railroads in the eastern portion of the United States. The time required to get from the Atlantic coast to the Pacific coast would be reduced to one week.

To plan was one thing, but actually to build the railroad was another. The Union Pacific had little difficulty recruiting Irish labor in the East, but in the West there were simply not enough people willing to work on the railroad. Many of those who had trekked across the continent or had sailed across the oceans were looking for more appealing ways of making their fortune. They were not interested in backbreaking labor. After two years, only 56 miles of track were laid by the Central Pacific, and the contract called for completion of the railroad in fourteen years.

In those days, there were no bulldozers or cranes or trucks. Everything had to be done by human hands. The tracks had to be laid across tall mountain ranges, across the burning sands of dry deserts, and across ravines and rivers with steep cliffs and swift-

In 8- to 12-foot-high snowdrifts, Chinese laborers struggled to keep the tracks open on the Central Pacific Railroad near Sacramento, California, in 1889.

Left: heavy machinery had not been invented in the 1860s. Track-laying required human muscles with the help of horses and carts. Without the Chinese laborers, completion of the transcontinental railroad would have been delayed considerably. The transcontinental railroad tied the nation together and brought about very rapid development and settlement of the West. The scene shown at right is San Francisco just over 100 years ago.

flowing waters. All the while the workmen had to fight off warring Indians who did not want "iron horses" running across their land.

The task of finishing the railroad seemed like an impossible dream until Charles Crocker, the construction boss, suggested that the Chinese might be able to do the work. At first everyone laughed at him because they thought the Chinese were too puny to be able to do such backbreaking work. However, a few were hired, and they did such a fine job that Crocker hired more and more. In fact, he even sent to China to recruit others, promising to pay their fare and a set wage for two or three years. The wages paid the Chinese were lower than those for whites. For example, the whites were paid $35 a month and were given meals and lodging, whereas the Chinese were paid $26 and no keep. Cheap labor costs, therefore, were a factor in the Chinese' becoming the main labor force on the Central Pacific, the western portion of the railroad.

With their picks and shovels, sledge hammers and straw baskets, the Chinese carved out narrow ledges on steep cliffs to lay the rails. They blasted tunnels through rock. They carted the dirt away in their straw baskets suspended from poles over their shoulders. They brought dirt in and leveled the railbeds. They braved sun and wind, rain and snow to lay thousands of miles of tracks starting at the Pacific Ocean to meet up with tracks being laid from the other end. By 1869, in record-breaking time, the railroad was completed. The construction of the United States transcontinental railroad is still considered the outstanding engineering feat of the century.

At first the people in the West were happy that the Chinese were there to do the type of work that they themselves did not care to do. By using Chinese labor, the West benefited from very rapid settlement and development. But after the railroad was completed in 1869, 25,000 men were thrown out of work at once.

All had to find new jobs. At the same time, more and more people arrived from the East because they could ride the new railroad. In the scramble for jobs, the Chinese were accused of working for low wages and taking away jobs from the white men.

KICK THEM OUT! When times were bad, it was very convenient to blame the Chinese. Their racial features were very different from those of white people. The Chinese men wore their hair in pigtails. They kept their native dress of loose cotton jackets, baggy trousers, and cloth shoes. They kept to themselves in the Chinese quarters and observed their own customs and traditions. They were looked upon as foreigners, although they were no more foreign than the other immigrants to the West. By playing upon the racial prejudices and fears of the whites, rabble-rousers portrayed the Chinese as evil and threatening.

Not only were the Chinese taunted and abused, they were attacked and their homes burned. Some were put on ships for China against their will. Others were taken to the outskirts of cities and forbidden to return. Many died because they had no food or shelter.

Special taxes against them in mining and fishing made it almost impossible for them to earn a livelihood. All kinds of laws were passed against them violating their rights under the U.S. Constitution. As business conditions became worse and worse, the cries that the Chinese must go became louder and louder.

In New York harbor, the Statue of Liberty, beckoning the poor and wretched to American shores, has always stood as a symbol of hope and freedom for immigrants coming from Europe. This statue, a gift from France, was dedicated in 1886. Few people realize that four years before that date the door to America had clanged shut in the face of the Chinese on the West Coast. In 1882, the U.S. government had passed a law stating that Chinese labor-

This fortune-teller earned his rice predicting the future for the Chinese in San Francisco around the year 1900. He may be consulting the *Book of Changes*, one of the Confucian classics, that tells people how to avoid misfortunes or how to take advantage of opportunities. This 3,000-year-old book has recently become popular for fortune-telling in the United States.

Above: leaders of the growing union movement found it easy to blame the Chinese for the bad times brought on by the depression of the 1870s. In the sandlots of San Francisco, they incite the people to chase the Chinese out of the country.

Right: massacre of the Chinese at Rock Springs, Wyoming. The homes of the Chinese were set on fire and the Chinese were shot as they tried to flee. Twenty-eight were killed and countless others injured.

THE CHINESE QUESTION.

During the 1870s, anti-Chinese feelings rose to a high pitch. This composite of pictures from the front page of the *Daily Graphic* of New York City shows how the Chinese were viewed at that time.

Left: later immigrants had already adopted the Western dress, and even sported the white caps in fashion in the United States at that time. Above: since the Chinese were not permitted to immigrate to the United States after 1882, all those who wanted to come in were suspected of trying to enter illegally and questioned closely in a prison-like place on Angel Island or Ellis Island.

ers were not permitted to enter the United States. Altogether, fourteen discriminatory laws were passed. These are known as the Chinese Exclusion Acts. Some Chinese, who had been here before and had gone out of the country temporarily, and even some American citizens with Chinese blood were locked up in places like Ellis Island or Angel Island and questioned for weeks or months before they were permitted to re-enter the country.

During this period the Chinese in this country lived in fear of the immigration officials. Many went back to China, and new immigrants could not enter. The population dropped from about 110,000 to almost half that number by 1920. The ones who stayed, huddled together in Chinatowns of the big cities like San Francisco, Los Angeles, New York, and Boston.

No matter how long a Chinese lived in the United States, he was not permitted to apply for citizenship. Up until the Civil War, only free white people were allowed to become naturalized citizens. The Fourteenth and Fifteenth Amendments to the constitution extended this right to black people. Since they were neither black nor white, the courts ruled that the Chinese were "aliens ineligible to citizenship."

The beautiful Pacific islands of Hawaii were not a part of the United States until 1898. Many Chinese had gone there to work on the sugarcane and pineapple plantations. The Hawaiians and Chinese were on very friendly terms, but when those islands became U.S. territory, all the discriminatory laws against the Chinese were put into effect in Hawaii as well.

CHINA-TOWNS In Chinatowns, the Chinese tried to hide from the American people and be as inconspicuous as possible. Since they felt unwanted in this country, they kept to their own ways, their own language, and their own customs. Job opportunities were very limited for them, and they had to take jobs such as doing housework, washing clothes, and cooking meals for other peo-

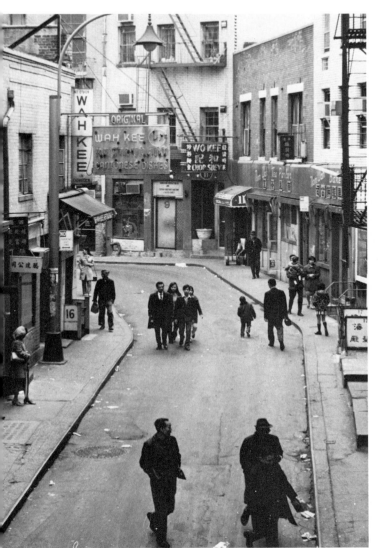

Left: colorful and exotic are the front streets of San Francisco's China-town. The curved tile roofs have a religious significance. If bad luck rains down from heaven, the curved eaves are supposed to deflect such misfortunes back upward. Above: the streets of New York's Chinatown are narrow and winding, built more than 100 years ago for horse-drawn carriages. Yet this area is one of the most densely populated in the entire city. Right: Doyer Street — the same place as in the adjoining photo in 1918. Most of these buildings are still standing today.

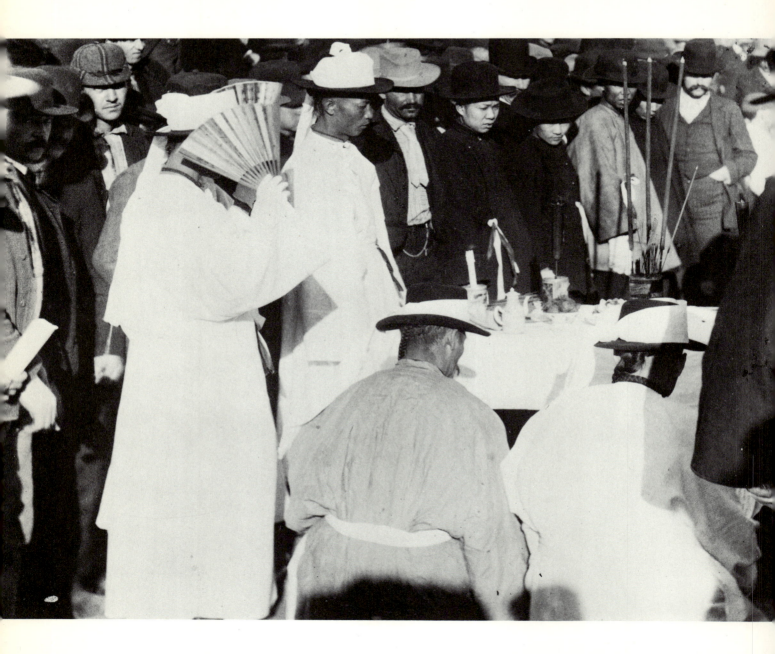

Mourners at a funeral service in 1891. Note that white is the color of mourning for near relatives of the dead. The deceased must have had many friends among the white men who came to pay their last respects.

ple. However, when they opened up eating places to serve their own countrymen, they attracted more white customers than Chinese. Chinese food is famous throughout the world for its taste and variety. Americans began to flock to the Chinese restaurants. They also wanted to buy the beautiful art objects made in China, such as carved ivories, shimmering silks, porcelain vases, scroll paintings, and jade ornaments. Gradually, Chinatowns became exciting places where tourists would visit, shop, and eat.

Behind the shops and restaurants, however, Chinatowns were self-contained communities, trying to meet the social needs of their people. The communities governed themselves by forming family organizations to help each other in case of need and to settle disputes and problems. These family groups then banded together to form an umbrella organization that governed the entire community. In San Francisco, this organization is known as the Chinese Six Companies. In other cities, it is known as the Chinese Benevolent Association.

Almost always, Chinatowns would be located in the poorer, run-down districts of the large cities. Because the Chinese did not trust white people or the government, they tried to keep to themselves. The more the Chinese tried to be hidden, the more mysterious they appeared in the eyes of the Americans.

FAMILIES BROKEN UP

The laws that did not permit Chinese to enter the country also prevented those who were here from sending for their families. Thus the Chinese in the United States were primarily men living a life of solitude. Since there was little to look forward to in this country, these people worked very hard, hoping to save enough money so that they could go back to China.

The laws that would not allow the Chinese into the country lasted for 61 years, from 1882 to 1943. As the group grew smaller and smaller, the Chinese were almost forgotten. Few people remembered the role the Chinese played in the development of the American West, or that there had been such a nationwide uproar over the ejection of a whole national group from American soil.

It was not until World War II that feelings against the Chinese changed. China and the United States were fighting on the same side against a common enemy — Japan. The American people were politically embarrassed that they had mistreated the Chinese, so they did away with the exclusion laws in 1943. But that did not mean any Chinese who wanted to could come in. The new law permitted only 105 persons of Chinese ancestry to come in each year. In comparison, Great Britain had a quota of 65,361, and Germany's quota was 25,814. With such a tiny quota, the Chinese population here remained very small and insignificant.

CHANGE IN IMMIGRA- TION LAWS
In 1965, more than 20 years later, the United States again changed its immigration laws. This time, immigrants were allowed to come in on a first-come, first-served basis instead of being admitted by the country you came from. Special preference, however, was given to family members and people with special skills and qualifications. The change meant that up to 20,000 Chinese could come in each year compared to 105 allowed in before. As a result, the new arrivals are different from the early Chinese forefathers, who were primarily laboring men.

Generally, today's newcomers are women and children being reunited with their husbands or fathers, or they are educated and specially trained people who are given preference to enter. Many are refugees. These refugees are people who had to flee China in the political struggle between the Nationalist government in Taiwan and the Communist government that came into power in Peking in 1949. Until President Nixon's visit to China in 1972, the United States insisted that Peking was not the rightful government of the Chinese mainland. The United States preferred to sup-

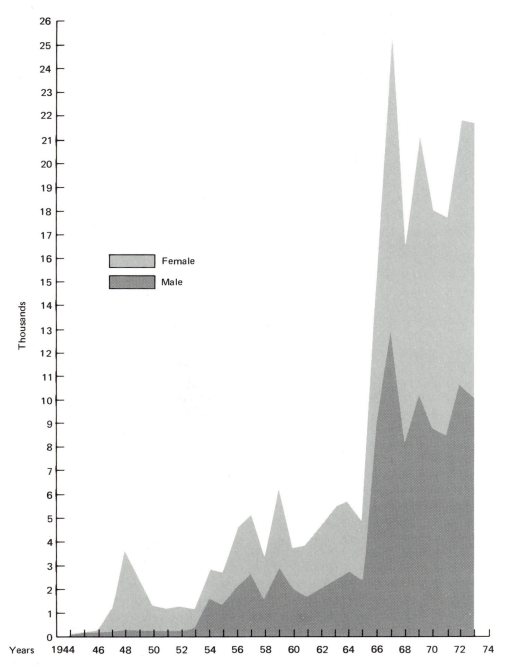

See how Chinese immigration went from almost nothing in 1944 to over 20,000 every year since 1965. It will be some time before these newcomers get used to life in this country.

port the Nationalists on the small island of Taiwan, which has another form of government. Even so, most of the Chinese who come to this country continue to originate from the mainland.

Since the Chinese had been kept out of the country for such a long time, and since most of those who were already here did not have their families with them, they rushed to apply for entry into the United States. On page 29 there is a chart showing how Chinese immigration jumped from the hundreds to the thousands in recent years.

The pie graph below shows the proportion of people from other lands who came to the United States in 1974. The black slice of the pie represents the Chinese. It is a fairly large slice of the whole pie. Still, the number of Chinese in the United States is a tiny portion of the total U.S. population.

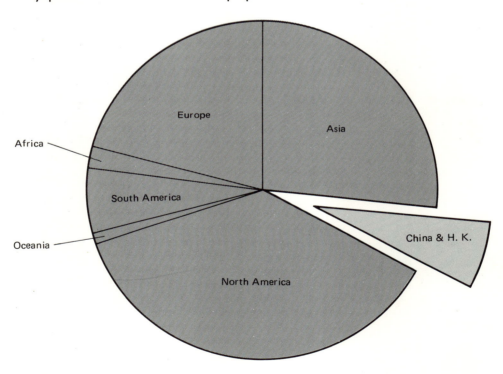

The small slice of the immigration pie for the year 1974 represents the Chinese.

GETTING USED TO THE UNITED STATES

For people who have to pull up roots and leave their homes and friends, going to a foreign land is a very painful experience. When they arrive in a new country, they want to live in a place where the faces and way of life will be similar to those they have left behind. That is why they are drawn to Chinatowns. However, the communities that served the Chinese when their numbers were small could not take in so many of the newcomers. These places were usually in the poorer sections of town where the buildings were very old and run-down. The former organizations could not handle the large numbers of new arrivals at once, either. Yet the immigrants continued to pour into these areas, pushing the boundaries of existing Chinatowns wider and wider.

Today's immigrants are better educated or have special skills. Their biggest problem is that many do not know how to speak, read, or write the English language. Therefore, they feel very helpless and are afraid to venture far from the community. To understand the feeling of these newcomers, imagine that your family has moved to China. Your parents would have to earn a living, although they spoke and understood no Chinese. Your family would have to get used to a Chinese-style house and to shopping in the open market, where you may never find bread, steak, breakfast cereals, or milk. These foods are not commonly eaten in China. Instead, you would have to get used to rice, salt fish, bitter melons, *bok choy*, and bean curd — foods common to the Chinese diet.

If you walked into a classroom where all your schoolmates looked different and wore clothes unlike your own, you would feel out of place. If the teacher started reading from a book that was written from top to bottom in little square characters like those on page 49, and if you could not make out one word that he or she was saying, you would feel very frustrated and unhappy until you were able to pick up a little of the Chinese language. If every time you spoke (in order to show that you were

Behind the fancy and gaudy gift shops, restaurants, and pagoda tops
of New York's Chinatown are soot-covered, rundown tenements. Some
of the buildings are over 100 years old. They have housed wave after
wave of immigrants — the Irish, Jews, Italians, Puerto Ricans, and now
the Chinese. This area in the Lower East Side bred social problems in
the past and continues to breed them in the present.

Right: a patient and under-standing teacher offers extra help to the student who may need special attention. Below: one of the biggest problems of the immigrant is having to learn a new language. This dedicated lady, Mitzie McKenzie, offers her services to tutor these men.

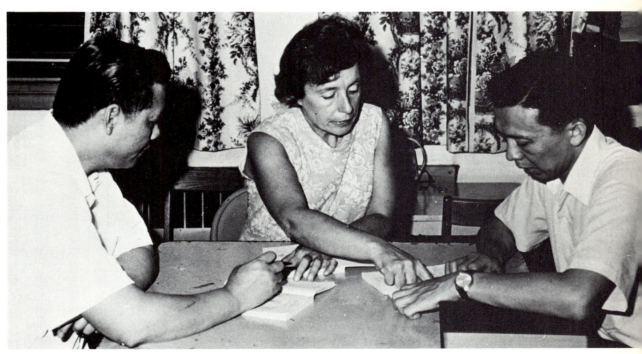

Right: loneliness, being left out, having no one to play with, are experiences common to Chinese American children, who are often not accepted among their school-mates. Above: learning a new language is especially hard work for this little girl, who just came from Hong Kong.

trying to learn the language and to prove that you could say a few words) your classmates laughed because you could not pronounce Chinese the way they did, you would feel very hurt. If your playmates made fun of you and would not let you join their games, you would feel very left out.

Similarly, Chinese children who come to this country face special problems. They have to get used to their new surroundings and to school. They have to try to make new friends. They have to spend more time at their homework. If they cannot speak or read well in English, their teachers may think they are stupid. If they cannot keep up, they may lose interest in school and drop out. Then they might spend their time in the streets and become troublemakers. Juvenile delinquency and gang activity, once a rare occurrence in the Chinese communities, is fast becoming a serious problem in Chinatowns today.

PRESERVING THEIR CULTURE

The idea that immigrants must get rid of their own language and customs as quickly as possible to become Americans is no longer encouraged. All the immigrant groups that have come to this country have brought with them rich folklore, customs, and ideas that have enriched American culture.

Wherever they have settled, the Chinese have tried to hold on to part of their rich and colorful heritage. Chinatowns are found in all parts of the world, and the community organizations preserve and hand down the Chinese way of life.

We already mentioned Chinese food, for instance. Not only have the Chinese preserved their eating habits, they have introduced them to the American people, so that Chinese food has become part of the American diet. Look on the supermarket shelves, and you will find proof of this statement.

One reason why Chinese food is so well liked is that it is very different from American and European food — not only the food

Right: to preserve their heritage, Chinese children stage performances of song and dance on festive occasions. Below: singing and playing on a Chinese stringed instrument. Ever since President Nixon's visit to China in 1972, there has been heightened interest in Chinese culture.

These three youngsters are practicing kung-fu, the age-
old method developed in China for self-defense. The little
girl seems to be holding her own against the two boys.

More and more young Chinese Americans are getting involved in community affairs. This young man and lady exhibit charts at a street fair to teach Chinatown residents the nutritional value of typical Chinese foods and vegetables.

itself, but also the way it is cooked and eaten. Have you ever eaten bamboo shoots or water chestnuts? They are very tasty and crunchy. Yet most Westerners do not use these foods. There are hundreds of items like these, blended into meats and vegetables, that give added flavor to Chinese dishes.

Historically, because of the scarcity of food in China, the people were forced to search every source for anything that could be eaten. For example, when they scraped the fungus growth from the bark of trees, they found that this mushroom-like plant was very flavorful. They gathered seaweeds washed ashore and tried various ways to cook them so that they would taste good.

The Chinese devote time and care to the preparation of their meals. They like to combine foods in a dish so that one food flavors the other. They pay extra attention to the way foods are cut so that they taste crunchy or smooth. A high fire or a low, simmering fire also affects the way food tastes. To the Chinese, eating is an important activity. They feel that cooking a meal is like painting a picture. A well-prepared meal is a work of art.

How is a Chinese meal served? Most people know that the Chinese eat with chopsticks instead of with knives and forks. Each person has a bowl of rice. The meat, vegetables, fish, or other dishes are placed in the center of the table. The food is cut up into bite-sized pieces. Each person picks up what he or she wants and eats it with rice.

Some of the foods that the Chinese enjoy eating are bean sprouts, snow peas, lotus root, ginger, *bok choy* cabbage, bean curd, shark's fins, and many, many others. The pastries are called *dim sum*, meaning "touch the heart." The varieties of these are as great as the imagination.

Sometimes the Chinese ways are quite different from the American. For example, in American society, the individual's concerns and rights are stressed. Boys and girls are encouraged from youth to be different, to speak up, to pursue their own interests. In the Chinese tradition, the well-being of the group comes first. In most

Above: framed against a wok on a cleaver and chopping board are Chinese broccoli, bok choy, winter melon, bean sprouts, bitter melons, and ginger roots. These fruits and vegetables are now grown in this country and form an important part of the Chinese American diet. Chinese food is not all the same. There are regional differences. Since most of the Chinese in this country come from the Canton area, Cantonese food is best known, but other cuisines like the Szechwan and Hunan are becoming popular. At left, a master chef creates a mouth-watering dish.

Dinner is eaten with chopsticks. The meat, soup, and vegetables are eaten with a heaping bowl of rice.

In China, this old woman might have been surrounded
by grandchildren, respected and honored by them.
In this country, she may be neglected and lonely.

instances, the group is the large kinship family, and every member of the family is expected to put its interests above his or her own.

For instance, members must conduct themselves so that they never disgrace their family name. Money earned belongs to the family and should be spent for the larger good of all its members. Family relations are obligated to help one another.

For centuries, marriage, the cornerstone of the family, was not a personal matter between a man and woman who fell in love. In most instances, the bride and groom were not even consulted and saw each other for the first time on their wedding day. Choosing a mate for their children was a duty of the parents, who were guided by the principle that a bride for their son or a groom for their daughter would carry on the family name in the best tradition. Some of these values and customs are no longer adhered to in China or the United States by the younger generations, although the older generations continue to hold on to the old traditions.

One of the most important traditions has been to honor one's parents and respect one's elders. The American culture emphasizes youth. More attention is paid to the young than to the old. For the elderly among the Chinese, this is a sad situation. In the past, they would have gone back to China to live out their remaining years in the home villages, where they would have been respected and honored. Here they seem to get in everybody's way. Many of the elderly can be seen sitting and gazing forlornly out of windows in Chinatown or whiling away their time on park benches from sun-up to sundown.

CHINESE FESTIVALS

The favorite festival for most Chinese people is New Year's. In fact, the occasion is many holidays rolled into one and is celebrated for a month. New Year's is not the first day in January of the Western calendar. The Chinese have their

The ceremonial Chinese dragon.

own calendar based upon the revolutions of the moon around the earth. The Western calendar is based upon the earth revolving around the sun. The first day of the Chinese year generally falls somewhere between the end of January and the first part of February according to the Western calendar.

The Chinese identify their years by a cycle of twelve animals. The years are supposedly governed by the characteristics of the animals. For instance, the Year of the Rat should be a bountiful year, because the Rat appears in the granary when the harvest has been good. The Year of the Rabbit should be a peaceful year. The twelve animals are: Rat, Ox, Tiger, Rabbit, Dragon, Snake, Horse, Sheep, Monkey, Rooster, Dog, and Pig.

If one were to count the Chinese years dating from the first emperor, 1977 would be the year 4,765.

Here is one youngster's version of how his family celebrates the holiday:

"My mother gets ready for the holiday more than a month ahead. She cleans the whole house from top to bottom. Then she decorates it with orange kumquat plants and sweet-smelling flowers. My father pastes happy sayings over the doorways written on red paper. Everything is red or orange. Red is a happy color.

"Mother makes all kinds of good foods to eat. My sister and I help her make fried doughballs with sesame seeds and black-bean fillings. She steams cupcakes that look like flowers in bloom. When they blossom out, that means we will have good fortune in the new year. If the cupcakes fall flat, that means bad luck. But Mother always takes extra care to see that the cupcakes rise.

"We all wear new clothes on New Year's Day. Mother and Father will give us a red envelope with money in it. They always say, 'Son, please behave better now that you are a year older.' I asked my parents why they say that, and they told me that New Year's Day is everybody's birthday, and everybody is a year older.

Youngsters dressed in blue jeans perform an ancient Chinese dragon dance.

On festive occasions, the Chinatown lion emerges to chase away evil spirits while firecrackers burst all around him. This celebration is for the American Bicentennial.

"On New Year's Eve, all of our relatives come over for a big dinner. We have roast duck and barbecued pork and all kinds of foods. Then my relatives give me good-luck money in a red envelope.

"We celebrate New Year's for a long time, not just one day. During that time, we all say nice things, and we all try to behave well. Mother and Father never scold or spank me during this period. There's a superstition that if you misbehave or get spanked during the New Year period, the same thing will happen to you all year long.

"The Sunday following, our family goes to Chinatown to set off firecrackers and watch the dragon dances. The noise is supposed to scare the evil spirits away. We visit all our relatives, and the children get red envelopes of money from the grown-ups. My cousins always have lots of firecrackers, and we go out into the streets to shoot them off."

Chinese New Year's is rich in folklore and customs. It is a time of joy and happiness, of giving and sharing, and of being with family and loved ones. A very important tradition is that all must settle their debts before the dawn of a new year so that they can start anew.

Other major festivals of the Chinese people are the Dragon Boat Festival and the Mid-Autumn Festival. The Dragon Boat Festival is observed in memory of a loyal minister Ch'u Yuan, who drowned himself when he was banished from his homeland. This festival falls on the fifth day of the fifth moon of the Chinese calendar. It is celebrated by boat races and by eating sticky rice cakes filled with meats, peanuts, egg yolks, and other ingredients wrapped in large bamboo leaves.

The Mid-Autumn Festival is somewhat like our Thanksgiving. It falls on the fifteenth day of the eighth month, when the harvest is over, and the people give thanks to the gods for their crops. It is also a day for fertility rites; the foods eaten are fruits and seeds. A traditional food is the moon cake, a thick round cake stuffed with candied fruits, watermelon seeds, crushed beans, or melon. This date is also remembered as an occasion for an uprising against a tyrannical emperor, when secret messages to revolt were enclosed and passed in the moon cakes.

The observance of these festivals serves to remind the Chinese in the United States of their heritage and to help them maintain their identity. However, these festivals are no longer celebrated as they were in China.

THE CHINESE LANGUAGE

The Chinese are very proud of their civilization and culture. Many parents send their children to Chinese school, so that they can learn the language and the history. Providing their children with the heritage of their past is like giving them the most valuable riches. And the key to these riches is the language.

At Chinese school, the students learn to read and write characters like the ones shown on page 49. Each character is a squarish-shaped one-syllable word. Chinese started out as a picture language. A picture was drawn to represent things or ideas. With more than 4,000 years of history, there is a rich body of literature written in the Chinese language.

People from all parts of the world have developed different ways of expressing themselves. There must be thousands of different ways of saying "dog," or "friend," or "eat." In the past, these differences came about because one group of people was separated from the others by tall mountains, by oceans, or by distance. Today these physical barriers no longer prevent people from moving from place to place more rapidly and more often. But when we say "friend" and the other person does not understand, then there is a language barrier. There is something in the way of our communicating, even though we are standing close together, face-to-face.

This is a page from a fourth grade reader. Chinese is written from right to left and from top to bottom.

Above right, below left: education is highly valued among the Chinese. According to the 1970 census, about 50 percent of all Chinese American males between ages 25 and 34 are college graduates. Above left: Chinese school is not always book learning. Right: new immigrants, who cannot speak English, are confined to jobs in Chinatown.

There are other ways that people get across their ideas. For instance, when people greet each other in the United States, they shake hands. The Eskimos rub noses. The French may kiss each other on both cheeks. The Chinese bow slightly and shake their own hands. These are the different customs that are a form of language. Americans may feel hurt or offended when they put out a hand to shake the hand of someone they have just met if the other person does not also put out a hand.

Body language is just as important a form of communication as words are. For instance, the Chinese smack their lips when they enjoy their food. Western manners insist that people eat quietly. The Chinese tend to control any outward expression of emotions such as joy or anger. Kissing and hugging a Chinese person may make him or her very uncomfortable and embarrassed. A Chinese tries not to disagree openly with or contradict a teacher or an elder for fear of causing that person to lose face.

New Chinese immigrants come to the United States with some of these cultural differences. They have to learn both a verbal language and an action language, and they have to learn them quickly in order to survive. In the Chinese community, their own people may help them because they understand the problem better. But when so many new immigrants come at once, the problems may become too much. After a while the situation will improve, but at the beginning the adjustment is a trying experience.

Chinese newspapers help the immigrants. These papers keep the Chinese informed about what is happening in their homeland, what is happening in their community, and what is happening on the American scene.

RELIGION The Chinese people are very tolerant in their beliefs. They do not necessarily worship a god, a Supreme Being, or supernatural force. Confucianism and Taoism are systems of beliefs built around a body of teachings that tell people

[52]

Left: worship of Buddha in China is an individual rite, but in this temple, located in the suburbs of New York City, the priests are leading their congregation in worship services. Note the stained-glass windows, which are more typical of Christian churches than Buddhist temples. Above: Reverend Eson Tse at the pulpit of the First Chinese Presbyterian Church in New York City.

Right: the younger-generation parent. (Father and son with balloon.) Below: many, many Chinese women now work in clothing factories.

how to live a good and moral life. Confucius and Lao-tzu, the founder of Taoism, were wise men who lived thousands of years ago. Tao means "the way." The ways of life taught by these two wise men were followed by the Chinese people into modern times.

Buddhism is a religion brought to China from India and Central Asia. Buddhists believe in an afterlife. Their god is Buddha. Some Chinese believe in one, or all, or none of these faiths. Christian missionaries also went to China, but Christianity did not attract many converts because it insisted that its followers believe in only one God.

In Chinatowns, however, there are many Christian churches. These churches offered the Chinese many valuable services. The missions set up health-care facilities and English language classes. The churches protected the Chinese against attacks. They spoke out against injustices. As a result, there are more Christian churches in Chinatown than there are Buddhist temples. The latter often attract more tourists than worshipers.

THE CHINESE AMERICAN FAMILY

In China, the individual is very much a part of the family group. But family means more than father, mother, and children. Family takes in a large group such as grandparents, uncles, aunts, cousins, brothers, sisters, and their husbands or wives and children. This is called a kinship family.

However, there were few families among the Chinese in the United States until the 1950s. Approximately nine out of ten of the early Chinese pioneers were young men, who came to make money. Then the laws passed against the Chinese did not allow them to bring in wives and children, so there were very few families here. The few were hold-overs from before the laws were passed. The men saw their wives and children only when they made an occasional trip to China. They did not do this very often because such trips were costly, and the journey was a long one.

Now that the laws have changed, many families are reunited in this country. But the Chinese family in the United States is quite different from that in China. One important change is that the wife or the mother generally works outside of the home. The type of work that most of these Chinese women do is sewing in the garment factories. They make skirts, jeans, pants, blouses, and dresses. They are paid by the piece. The rates are very low, so they have to work long, hard hours. Some of the women take their younger children to the factory with them. The older children are often left with no one to supervise them when they come home from school.

There may be little family life because the parents are working hard to pay off expenses of coming to the United States and having to start life over again. Families no longer live together as a kinship group. The younger generation may move to the suburbs, while the older Chinese prefer staying in Chinatowns.

A huge gap is arising between the children and their parents. The children pick up English and American customs very quickly. The parents prefer to cling to the ways in which they were brought up in China. Which ways are better? The parents think the old is better. The children like the new. Often the parents cannot control their children. The children look for a group to relate to. Some may join neighborhood gangs.

The young people are frustrated too. They hardly know their parents, who are working from morning to night. They may live in crowded quarters in a Chinatown with little or no recreational facilities. They may be confused about whether to follow the teachings of their parents when these teachings do not seem appropriate to their lives in the United States. They need help, but do not know where to turn.

In their anger and frustration, they are banding together to organize and protest. Unlike their parents' generation, which remained silent, the younger generations are making themselves heard.

Newly arrived immigrants, still wearing their Chinese jackets, (right) feel a bit unsure of themselves in the milling crowds of a schoolyard. These Chinese children (above) like to play baseball too, but there are no playing fields in the back alleys of Chinatown.

Left: the Chinese are now beginning to stand up for their rights. Peter Yew, a young college student, was allegedly beaten by the police when he protested against mistreatment of another Chinese by a white man. In anger, the Chinese community staged one of the most massive demonstrations ever seen in New York City in 1975. Ten thousand people marched against the police precinct and then on to City Hall to protest the manhandling of Peter Yew.

These children attend a Chinese school in San Francisco's Chinatown. Schools like this one were set up and run by the community because the parents did not want their children bused out of town to public schools.

WHERE THE CHINESE LIVE

Most of the Chinese in this country are found along the coastal states of California and New York and in the Pacific island state of Hawaii. They tend to cluster together in large urban centers like San Francisco, Los Angeles, Honolulu, and New York City. They live in every state in the Union, but in the central states there may be no Chinese face visible for miles around.

Every ten years, the United States government counts the number of people in this country. This count is called a census. In 1970, the census counted 435,000 Chinese. Since that time, however, many more have come in as immigrants. By 1980 there may be 750,000. Nevertheless, the Chinese are still a very small minority.

THE WORK THEY DO

Most Americans have fixed ideas about what work the Chinese do in this country. They think the Chinese are still working at the same kinds of jobs they used to work at in the past. In stories, television, and advertisements, the Chinese usually appear as servants, laundrymen, waiters or bartenders, or as evil criminals.

These ideas are not true. The new immigration laws are changing the makeup of people who are permitted to come to this country. Those who are better educated or have special skills get first preference. That is why there are many scientists, merchants, doctors, nurses, and teachers among the Chinese. One big problem for these people is that they have to get used to new ways of doing things. Perhaps they cannot speak English. Then they have trouble finding the type of job that they would like to have in their field of training or education.

More and more Chinese are going into jobs that demand in telligence and advanced training like engineering and teaching. Such jobs are called professions. Many Chinese are in the pro-

CONGRATULATIONS MARCH FONG
SECRETARY OF STATE OF CALIFORNIA

From upper left: Norman Lau Kee is sworn into office as Commissioner of Human Rights. The Chinese have begun to take an increasing interest in U.S. politics. General Dewey Kwoc Kung Lowe is the first person of Chinese ancestry promoted to the rank of general in the Air Force. He is a much-decorated command pilot, with the Legion of Merit and the Distinguished Flying Cross among his many awards and honors. Since this photo was taken, he has been promoted to major general. The Chinese community shared March Fong's honor when she was sworn in as secretary of state of California in 1975.

From upper left: Senator Hiram Fong and Mrs. Fong. The life story of the senator goes from the slums of Kaliki to the halls of the U.S. Senate, where he served Hawaii for three terms. Bruce Lee popularized the Chinese martial arts called kung-fu on American motion-picture screens. The image of him as a fearless fighter made him an idol to thousands of Chinese American youths. Connie Chung's face and voice are familiar to millions of people who see or hear her almost daily on CBS-TV or radio. As their Washington reporter, she covers the White House and Congress. Judge Harry W. Low, first Chinese American to preside over the Superior Court in California. He now sits in the same chambers where some of the harshest anti-Chinese laws were passed.

fessions. However, a large number of the men are also found in restaurant work and a large number of the women in garment factories. Often both parents must work to earn enough to support the family.

It is only within the past ten or twenty years that opportunities have opened up to the Chinese in this country to work at jobs other than lowly ones, but quite a number have used their new-found opportunities to good advantage. Some have managed within this short period of time to distinguish themselves or to make meaningful contributions.

The Chinese were among the early pioneers who helped develop the American West. Their treatment by this nation is a shameful chapter in American history. They did not begin to immigrate to this country again until recent years because they had been denied admittance by U.S. laws. Today the Chinese make up a good proportion of our new immigrants. These people have brought with them the teachings of an ancient civilization and a colorful culture. Because they are such a newly uprooted group, they have to work extra hard to adjust to their new life in this country.

INDEX *The page numbers in italics indicate illustrations.*

ABOUT THE AUTHOR Professor Betty Lee Sung teaches at The City College of the City University of New York in the Department of Asian Studies, where she has started a new field of study about Asians in the United States. Her first book, *Mountain of Gold* (republished in paperback under the title *The Story of the Chinese in America*) has become a standard work for ethnic studies courses. Professor Sung is an American-born Chinese who has lived and studied in China and the United States. She speaks three Chinese dialects, which helps her work and research in the Chinese communities. Professor Sung lives with her family in Douglaston, New York.